About This Book

Title: *Dig It!*

Step: 2

Word Count: 121

Skills in Focus: R-blends

Tricky Words: people, machine, bulldozer, over, dirt, build, fence, concrete, structures, use, hole, hold

Ideas for Using This Book

Before Reading:

- **Comprehension:** Look at the title and cover image together. Walk through the pictures in the book with readers and have them make predictions about what they might learn while reading. Help them make connections by asking what they already know about machines that dig.
- **Accuracy:** Practice saying the tricky words listed on page 1.
- **Phonemic Awareness:** Explain to the readers that a blend is two consonants together that each make a sound. Discuss that some blends include the letter *r*. Read aloud story words containing r-blends, beginning with *truck*. Slowly say each of the sounds in the word and have the students call out the word. Call attention to each blend and where it is found within the word. Other words to practice include *grab*, *drop*, *tracks*, *grip*, and *strong*.

During Reading:

- Have readers point under each word as they read it.
- **Decoding:** If readers are stuck on a word, help them say each sound and blend the sounds together smoothly. You may want to point out r-blends as they appear.
- **Comprehension:** Invite students to talk about what new things they are learning about machines while reading. What are they learning that they didn't know before?

After Reading:

Discuss the book. Some ideas for questions:

- Have you seen any construction machines before? What kinds?
- What do you still wonder about machines that dig?

Dig It!

Text by Marley Richmond

Reading Consultant
Deborah MacPhee, PhD
Professor, School of Teaching and Learning
Illinois State University

PICTURE WINDOW BOOKS
a capstone imprint

People use
machines to build.

They can dig, drop, dump, grab, and drill.

A bulldozer digs.
It has tracks.

Tracks help it go
over bumps and dips.

Tracks help the bulldozer grip land.

A dump truck has a bed.

Another truck drops dirt in the bed.

The dump truck takes trips to dump the dirt.

This machine can grab and grip.

It crams logs on a truck.

A man is building a fence. He digs up grass. He drills.

Then he puts a log in the hole. He props it up.

Next he adds concrete.
It drips from a drum.

It will hold the log strong.
This will be a fence.

Machines help us build structures that are small or grand.

More Ideas:

Phonemic Awareness Activity

Practicing R-Blends:

Tell readers they will slowly say each of the sounds of story words containing r-blends. Say an r-blend word for the readers to repeat. They will slowly stretch out the sounds of each word, tapping the table as they produce each sound.

Suggested words:

- truck
- drill
- grab
- trips
- tracks
- drop

Extended Learning Activity

Build a Machine:

Machines can dig up dirt. But they can help with other jobs too. Have readers think about what kind of machine they would like to have. Ask readers to draw their ideas. Then ask them to write a few words or sentences about what job their machine would help them do. Challenge readers to use words with r-blends in their descriptions.

Published by Picture Window Books, an imprint of Capstone
1710 Roe Crest Drive, North Mankato, Minnesota 56003
capstonepub.com

Copyright © 2026 by Capstone.
All rights reserved. No part of this publication may be reproduced in whole or in part, or stored in a retrieval system, or transmitted in any form or by any means, electronic, mechanical, photocopying, recording, or otherwise, without written permission of the publisher.

Library of Congress Cataloging-in-Publication Data is available on the Library of Congress website.

ISBN: 9798875277221 (hardback)
ISBN: 9798875277184 (paperback)
ISBN: 9798875277160 (eBook PDF)

Image Credits: Getty: filonmar, 1, 6, GKV, 22–23; Shutterstock: Alex Stemmer, front cover, Bjorn Heller, 7, Budimir Jevtic, 20, Gustavo Pereira Castro, 14–15, Juan Enrique del Barrio, 5, 24, Kletr, 4, back cover, LETOPISEC, 8–9, MagioreStock, 2–3, Parilov, 10–11, seroma72, 12–13, ungvar, 18, 19, 21, Vladimir Mulder, 16–17

Printed and bound in China. PO 6460